COLLECTABLE
TEDDY BEARS

Design: Stonecastle Graphics Ltd
Photography: Neil Sutherland
Editor: Nicola Dent

CLB 3361
Published by Grange Books
an imprint of Grange Books Limited
The Grange, Grange Yard, London SE1 3AG
© 1994 CLB Publishing
Godalming, Surrey
All rights reserved
Printed and bound in Singapore
Published in 1994
ISBN 1-85627-420-9

COLLECTABLE
TEDDY BEARS

Grange BOOKS

Arctophily

*A*rctophily is the name that has been given to the fascinating hobby of collecting teddy bears, while *arctophile* describes the avid collector. The term, literally meaning love or friend of bears, comes from the Greek words *arktos*, bear, and *philos*, friend.

A Hug of Bears

*A*s with groups of animals, a collection of teddy bears now also has its own specific name: a *hug*. This descriptive word originates from the late British actor Peter Bull, a keen arctophile and author of *Bear with Me* and *The Teddy Bear Book*, two titles which, in 1969, sparked off a revival in teddy bear interest.

9

Teddy Title

In any book on teddy bears the origin of this popular toy's name comes up at one point or another. In fact, the story is confused and there is more than one explanation of what, or who, inspired the word *teddy bear*.

Some say this appealing toy was named after King Edward VII of England – affectionately known as Ted – who, a frequent visitor to the zoo, was reputed to take a particular interest in the bear.

More commonly, historians state that the name came from Theodore (Teddy) Roosevelt, America's twenty-sixth president, who refused to shoot a bear cub that was tied to a tree during an unsuccesful hunting expedition in 1902. Political cartoonist Clifford Berryman of *The Washington Post* captured this event in a cartoon entitled 'Drawing the Line in Mississippi', from which stemmed the description 'Teddy's Bear'.

Teddy bears and location courtesy Museum of Childhood, Ribchester

11

Earliest and Oldest

Dating from 1903, 'Teddy's Bear' and 'Friend Petz' are the oldest bears to exist, although no one is quite sure which was the first to be made.

The former was the creation of Morris Michtom, inspired by the infamous cartoon of President 'Teddy' Roosevelt confronting a tiny bear cub. Michtom sent his teddy bear to the President with an appeal to use this powerful figure's name for the new stuffed toy. His request was granted and the designer went on to establish the successful Ideal Novelty and Toy Company. Today, Teddy's Bear can be found in the Smithsonian Institute, America.

It is widely believed, however, that Friend Petz may have been the earlier of the two teddy bears. This toy was designed by Richard Steiff, nephew of Margarete Steiff, the woman who founded Steiff & Co, the world's most famous teddy bear and toy company. No interest was shown in the new toy until the 1903 Leipzig Toy Fair when, on the last day, a buyer for a large American store placed an order for 3,000 bears. Friend Petz is now on display in the Giengen Steiff offices, Germany.

To help prevent fraud, the distinctive *Knopf im Ohr* or Button in Ear trademark – as seen attached to this fairly new, white bear – was introduced by Steiff & Co in 1905.

13

Original Teddies

Fur, stuffings, body shape, eyes and facial features are all ways of estimating the approximate age of your teddy bear. The first bears were stuffed with straw or excelsior, a material made of long, fine wood shavings that was used as the packing material for shipping fragile objects! Fur was created from mohair plush, an imitation of real animal hair that uses the silky wool of the Angora goat. The first teddies were shaped more like the wild bear on which they were modelled – taller and leaner, with long arms, moveable arms and heads, a hump and a protruding muzzle; some were even designed to stand on all fours, although these were less popular. Boot-buttons tended to be used for eyes, and noses and mouths were hand-stitched.

A change in both stuffing and overall shape has resulted in teddies becoming rounder, softer and ultimately more huggable. Mohair plush is increasingly replaced by less expensive synthetic furs and, in order to satisfy the strict safety regulations that now exist, firmly attached glass or plastic eyes have frequently replaced boot-buttons, and noses are fashioned from rubber or plastic.

One aspect that has hardly changed over the years is that both early and new teddy bears almost always stand upright, unlike their natural counterpart in the wild. Some say this has increased the teddy bear's lasting popularity as it helps to emphasize the human characteristics of the animal!

Teddy bears and location courtesy
Museum of Childhood, Ribchester

15

Talking Bears

Modern teddies often come equipped with music boxes and even tape recorders, but in early incarnations they mostly just growled. The voice boxes, called *growlers*, began as an oilcloth bellows with a lead weight to open and close it. The rush of air passed through a cardboard tube fitted with a reed that made a growling sound whenever the bear was tilted. In another version, the bear's inner parts included an oilcloth balloon that pushed air across a reed when he was punched in the stomach. Who wouldn't growl if they were hit like that?!

Once marvelled at, the teddy bear growler has since been superseded by the technobears of today, whose abilities have become more and more complex. Teddy bears can laugh, whistle, play music or, by means of a concealed microchip, speak more than 400 words. Some even have eyes that light up when they recognize a familiar voice!

17

First Bears

Everyone is concerned about the happiness of a newborn baby and certain studies have indicated that, with over half the parents questioned, a teddy was the child's favourite toy.

It is generally suggested that the teddy must not be larger than the child to whom he is given, as too large a size would make the bear hard to cuddle thereby losing some companionship. As for clothes, which have become popular marketing tools in the teddy bear world, the first bear a young babe owns should be as naked as a newborn to get all the benefits possible from his soft furry coat.

Despite doctors' orders about cleanliness it is best not to wash the teddy too frequently as this furry companion will acquire the scent of both the infant and mother – smells that further enhance the reassurance it can provide.

In recent years an American 'Rock-a-bye-Bear' and an Australian version 'Sleepy Bear' have been designed and, with the maternal, pulse-like sound they produce, have proved a great success in helping to comfort and soothe young babies.

But above all, remember that never, ever, should a teddy bear be relegated to a nursery shelf. Bears have feelings, too!

19

Good Bears

One psychiatrist has been quoted as saying teddies represent goodness, benevolence and kindliness to children. Possibly more than any other toy, the teddy plays an invaluable role in helping with abused, traumatized, and hurt children. In 1973, an international fund-raising organization known as 'Good Bears of the World' was set up by American James T. Ownby in order to provide bears for suffering children and the forgotten elderly. On the 27th October of each year – the birthday of the late Teddy Roosevelt – Good Bear Day is celebrated to help raise funds.

Specific bears have also often been used to promote charities such as Britain's 'Children in Need' and 'Help the Sick Kids' appeals, and are also frequently used as mascots for hospitals that include the Children's Hospital of Orange County in Disneyland, U.S.

Today, many specialized bears have been designed for individuals with complaints that range from allergies and sensitivity to chemicals to heart problems and speech defects. A special 'signing bear' – in the form of a puppet in which the teacher can guide the hands – and a teddy whose eyes light up in recognition of a familiar voice, have both been developed to encourage deaf children to speak. With the general increase in technology, the existence of more complex, 'talented' and useful bears has become an area that is growing rapidly.

21

Literary Cele-bear-ties

Most countries have their own national bear 'heroes' made famous from their appearance in books, in comic strips or on television. Among the earliest teddy bears to make a literary appearance were Seymour Eaton's successful Roosevelt Bears, whose adventures delighted millions of young readers. Brought to life in 1905, sadly Teddy G and Teddy B are almost unknown today, except to collectors. Their message, however, is still quite valid to teach children that animals, even bears, may have some measure of human feeling.

Certain fictional bears have been inspired by specific teddy bears. In 1956, Michael Bond found a lonely teddy in London's Paddington Railway Station and went on to write about a marmalade-loving bear in a duffel coat who had arrived there from Peru with a plaintive note attached, reading 'Please look after this bear. Thank you'. Also based on a real teddy bear that was a gift to his son, was A.A. Milne's Winnie-the-Pooh, perhaps internationally the best-known bear character of all time. The amusing exploits of this cuddly, honey-loving teddy have been translated into over twenty languages, including Classical Greek and Latin.

Teddy bears have also featured in adult literature, with possibly the most famous being Aloysius, the bear who appears in Evelyn Waugh's novel *Brideshead Revisited* and – captured in verse – British Poet Laureate Sir John Betjeman's teddy bear, Archibald.

23

Artist Bears

With the record sum of £55,000 attained at a Christie's auction for a 1930s Steiff bear, collecting teddy bears has become an even more serious business, and sometimes a worthwhile investment financially as well as sentimentally!

A rapidly growing area in the teddy bear world is that of special, limited-edition teddies created by individual designers or 'artists', rather than by large manufacturers. Many of these *artist bears* are based on certain themes, on specific events, or on famous figures, William Shakesbear, Bjorn Bearg, Elvis Bear and Robin Hood and Maid Marion bears, to name but a few. Christopher Columbear was created to celebrate the centenary of Columbus first discovering America, while the Titanic Bear commemorates the tragic sinking of the mighty liner *Titanic* and is modelled on Gatti, the teddy that survived this disaster.

Both unusual and imaginative, artist bears have the advantage that each is very personal, and being handmade, unique.

25

Teddy Songs

The popular 'Teddy Bear's Picnic' is undoubtedly the most well-known teddy song to exist. American composer John Bratton wrote the music and had hoped that it would become the official campaign song for Theodore 'Teddy' Roosevelt in the 1908 election, only to be disappointed when T.R. stepped aside in favour of William Howard Taft. In 1930, to accompany the music, British songwriter Jimmy Kennedy wrote the renowned lyrics:

'If you go down
in the woods today....'

Many other songs featuring teddy bears in their words have since been written; another famous song being Elvis Presley's 'Teddy Bear', which he sang in the 1957 film *Loving You*. For a long time after the release of the film Elvis was literally inundated with teddy bears sent from hundreds of admiring fans!

27

Bears in the Fast Lane

Many stories have been told about adventurous bears who have accompanied their owners to war, on exciting journeys, and even on record-breaking events. Among these teddies are Mr. Woppit – who was with his owner Donald Campbell during the setting of world land and water speed records – and the teddy mascot who was with pioneer female aviator Amy Johnson when she became the first woman to fly solo from Britain to Australia.

A Hamley's teddy bear is reputed to have been used to test the first parachute prototype, while both Senior Under Officer Edward Bear and his successor Officer Cadet Edward Bear have both jumped with the British RMAS Parachute Club, for whom they are the mascot! A mascot for another British regiment is Sopwith Bear, pictured here, who for many years was the faithful companion of his RAF pilot owner. The London Fire Brigade had a bear mascot during World War II and other teddies are believed to have saved their owner's lives during the war by intercepting bullets!

And the list of courageous teddy bears goes on…!

29

Active Bears

Teddy bears often take pride of place as the mascot for various sporting teams, as well as for the individual athlete, and have been the loyal companion of many a celebrity.

In the 1980 Summer Olympic Games held at Moscow, Russia, the mascot was a bear called Mishka. And, although not strictly speaking a member of the bear family, Australia's appealing koala Billy Bluegum was considered the unofficial mascot of the Olympic Games held at Melbourne in 1956.

In the adventurous sporting world of climbing, bears have even been taken mountaineering! Tiny Zissi the Bear faithfully accompanied Italian Alpine climber Walter Bonatti in 1965, when he scaled the North Face of the Matterhorn!

31

A Working Bear

The inspiration for the 1902 Berryman cartoon was Theodore Roosevelt's refusal to shoot an unprotected bear cub. The figure of a bear was subsequently adopted by the U.S. Forest Service as a symbol for the prevention of forest fires and named Smokey.

In 1950, a bear cub that had survived a forest fire was taken to Washington Zoo and became the living embodiment of Smokey. After twenty-five years of faithful service promoting the slogan 'Remember, Only You Can Prevent Forest Fires', Smokey was retired to a ranch at Carson National Forest in New Mexico.

Smokey has appeared on numerous posters and advertising campaigns and, in America, has practically become a household name. Many Smokey bear teddies have been based on this loveable figure and a *Smokey the Bear* club has been established to encourage young people to care for their environment.

33

Shaggy Dog Story

Not just a child's best friend, the teddy bear has constantly proved to be the much loved and loyal companion of many an adult and even, as the following story illustrates, of a domestic pet!

A champion show dog from New Orleans, according to a tale his owner swore was true, had been raised with a bear cub and was quite attached to it. When the bear died, the dog lost not only his zest for life, but his ability to win prizes. One day, when out for a walk, the dog fell deeply in love with a stuffed bear in a store window. He refused to move from the spot and his owner was forced to buy the bear. From that moment, the dog's life changed. He was a champion again, thanks to the teddy bear, which he carried everywhere in his mouth, even to dog shows. It is not recorded, however, whether the teddy bear himself was ever awarded any prizes, although he surely deserved one!

35

Bear Care

As most teddy owners know, taking care of your teddy bear is of the utmost importance. After all, how many times has your teddy bear taken care of you? In 1954 Wendy Boston created a revolutionary new, machine-washable teddy bear, but on the whole most bears are fairly delicate and require more sensitive treatment.

As a general rule, try to keep your bear out of direct sunlight and dusty, smoky or damp atmospheres, and away from drafts, water pipes, air conditioners and humidifiers, as these conditions could mar your teddy's fur. Use lavender bags, cedar wood shavings or mothballs to protect the coat from moths, who are inclined to find fur quite tasty!

When cleaning your bear begin by removing any dust by gently applying a vacuum, covered with cloth to cushion the suction. Before washing always first test any cleansing substance on a small section of your bear that is hidden from sight, such as under the arm, to ensure that it does not alter the colour or texture of the fur. Use soapsuds – rather than soapy liquid – from a mild detergent or upholstery cleaner and apply with a soft-bristled brush or toothbrush. Never scrub your bear, but gently wipe the foam away. Avoid mouth, nose and paws as these areas may not be colourfast. Sit your bear in the sun to dry or use a hairdryer on a low setting and then gently comb the fur to remove any tangles.

37

Bears and Food

*'Honey can be runny, or really very thick,
But full of taste and oh so sweet,
It's every bear's best treat!'*

Even the *Encyclopaedia Britannica* states that bears love honey and it is true to say that most teddy bear characters are portrayed as being very attached to their food!

Mishka, the Russian bear, has been described as 'desperate' to open a pot of honey he found in the forest, and Seymour Eaton's Roosevelt Bears had an astonishing capacity for anything edible! Paddington Bear is constantly preoccupied with his marmalade sandwiches, a handy supply of which he keeps under his hat, while Winnie-the-Pooh is always on the look out for honey or something edible as 'elevenses'!

Gingerbread Bears

Makes 20-25 biscuits

*500g/1lb plain flour
2 tsps ground ginger
1 tsp mixed spice
2 tsps bicarbonate of soda
120g/4oz butter
120g/4oz soft brown sugar
90g/3oz black treacle
60g/2oz golden syrup
1 egg, beaten*

Preheat oven to 180°C/350°F/Gas Mark 4. Mix together the dry ingredients. Melt butter, sugar, treacle and syrup and pour onto the dry ingredients. Add the egg and mix to form a dough. Knead lightly and roll out to 0.3cm/1/8-inch thick. Use a cutter to make as many teddy shapes as possible. Bake in the oven for 20 minutes or until lightly browned. When cool, decorate with raisins or icing.

Bear-o-scopes

Although most bears join their families at Christmas, which would make them Capricorns, the first teddy of record appeared in a newspaper cartoon by Clifford Berryman on November 18, 1902, which would make his birth sign Scorpio, or possibly on the cusp between Scorpio and Sagittarius, two very auspicious signs of the Zodiac.

Just as we have birthdays, every teddy bear also has his or her individual birthday, some bears even arriving with a birth certificate attached to help you recall their particular bear-o-scope!

AQUARIUS
21 JAN – 18 FEB
PISCES
19 FEB – 19 MAR

ARIES
20 MAR – 20 APR

TAURUS
21 APR – 21 MAY

GEMINI
22 MAY – 21 JUN

40

CANCER
22 JUN – 22 JUL

LEO
23 JUL – 23 AUG

VIRGO
24 AUG – 23 SEPT

LIBRA
24 SEPT – 23 OCT

SAGITTARIUS
23 NOV – 21 DEC

SCORPIO
23 OCT – 22 NOV

CAPRICORN
22 DEC – 20 JAN

Teddy Bear Gatherings

Today, teddy bear picnics, fairs, festivals and conventions have become a widespread event in many a country and are so popular that it seems they must be based on centuries-old tradition. But they are, in fact, a relatively recent phenomenon.

Possibly the first gathering of any real significance was the British 'Great Teddy Bear Rally and Honey Fair' held at Longleat, the stately English home of the Marquis of Bath and his teddy Clarence. Thousands of teddy bears and owners turned up to celebrate the occasion, which has since been repeated.

All over the world teddy clubs and societies – and also several teddy bear publications – have been established to provide teddy information and news and the opportunity to meet other keen collectors and arctophiles.

43

ACKNOWLEDGEMENT
The publishers would like to thank the following for providing
teddy bears, props and locations for photography:

Colour Box Miniatures, Lauder, Berwickshire
The Cotswold Teddy Bear Museum, Broadway
London Toy and Model Museum, London
Museum of Childhood, Ribchester
Preston Manor, Brighton,
courtesy of Brighton Borough Council
Ian Pout, Teddy Bears of Witney